ARTHURIAN SITES
IN THE WEST

C. A. RALEGH RADFORD
DLitt, FBA, FSA, FRHistS

MICHAEL J. SWANTON
PhD, FSA, FRHistS

University of Exeter
English Medieval Studies

ISBN 0 85989 026 0

Printed in Great Britain by
The Printing Unit of the University of Exeter
Devon

CONTENTS

LIST OF ILLUSTRATIONS

PLATES

PREFATORY NOTE

THIS BOOKLET was prepared on the occasion of the eleventh triennial conference of The International Arthurian Society, meeting at Exeter in August 1975. Our object was to provide a brief guide to major West Country sites where traditional association with Arthurian legends has been measured against the objective yardstick of archaeological investigation. We are grateful to friends and colleagues whose ready co-operation made its preparation the easier, notably: Professor Leslie Alcock, Mr P. A. Rahtz and Professor Charles Thomas. And for permission to reproduce illustrations we are indebted to the following: Bryan Whitton (Figs. 3,7,16), Charles Woolf (Pl. II), Aerofilms Ltd. (cover illus., Pl. III), Cambridge University Collection per Professor J. K. S. St Joseph (Pl. I), Camelot Research Committee (Pl. IV), The Controller of Her Majesty's Stationery Office (Fig. 2), Council for British Archaeology (Fig. 1, map), Royal Archaeological Institute (Fig. 12).

I

THE 'ARTHURIAN' WEST

THE 170-MILE peninsula which extends from the ancient Forest of Selwood to Lands End is a region of marked geographical contrasts. There are extensive upland areas of grass and heather moorland like Dartmoor, Exmoor and Bodmin Moor, as well as lower rolling hills and fertile, well-watered river valleys. Much of the coastline is rocky and well-provided with deep estuaries. The prevailing winds are westerly; the climate mild and relatively moist, suitable to the maintenance of herds and dairy-farming rather than grain production. Mineral ores: tin, copper, iron, lead and silver, are relatively abundant, and were all exploited in Roman times and later. Towards the end of the Roman period there were changes in relative land and sea levels which brought the sea at the highest tides to almost the 20 foot contour. As a result, drowned river valleys and even deeper estuaries formed fine natural harbours and allowed easy access to the hinterland. To the north-east of the region the Somerset Levels must have been at least sporadically swamped, forming a large area of fen and marsh-land extending for over 20 miles inland between the Mendips and Quantocks. And this, together with the Forest of Selwood, will have formed a natural barrier to the east. Land communications east-west down the length of the peninsula must have been relatively difficult. Major Roman roads were few, and travel would have been easiest by water, either coastwise, or up and down the major estuaries and rivers made more navigable by the rise in sea level.

The degree to which the native population had been Romanised seems to have varied considerably down the length of the peninsula. Indeed, little Romanisation at all occurred outside towns such as Exeter (ISCA) and Bath (AQUAE SULIS). During the later third century a group of wealthy landowners built fine courtyard villas and brought a high style of Romanised, and later Christianised, living within reach of the cosmopolitan spa at Aquae Sulis. But further west, there is no evidence that Isca ever gave rise to a similar pleiad of villa life. And though long evicted by the legions from their defended hillforts, the native population held to a conservative manner of life, continuing to build small groups of simple round huts.

In the last years of direct Roman rule the wealthy Somerset landowners seem to have moved to the greater safety of the newly fortified towns, leaving their estates in the hands of native bailiffs with simpler tastes. Some may have left Britain altogether. One young noblewoman (*clarissima femina*) from Devonshire (*civis Dumnonia*) is known to have died at Split on the Adriatic coast of Yugoslavia in the year 425. The towns of the West Country seem to have survived as organised communities for much longer than those in the areas of Germanic settlement further to the east. In the west the main danger came from Irish raiding parties who, unlike the Anglo-Saxon invaders, do not seem to have been intent on seizing the land. But although there can be little doubt that towns like Exeter remained useful commercial centres, they had probably ceased to exercise any extensive administrative function long before 410 when the Roman Emperor Honorius wrote telling the *civitates* of Britain to look after their own defence. Already by the end of the fourth century, six inches of black mould covered the floor of what was probably the Exeter forum; while at Aquae Sulis the unserviced drainage system had collapsed, waterlogging the entire baths area. The defence of both town and country was now entrusted to locally-raised home-guard units rather than regular military detachments. And it would appear that shadowy kingdoms of an almost pre-Roman type had emerged in the west at least one generation before the official end of central Roman administration and the beginning of Britain becoming once more responsible for its own affairs.

But far from being isolated during the post-Roman phase, the south-western peninsula, remote and backward during Roman times, now experienced a period of renaissance as a result of renewed contacts with the outside world. The communities of the far west of Britain are linked in a very real way by the Atlantic sea-routes. And, as reflected in the *Lives* of the Celtic saints, the south-western peninsula occupies a focal situation in the western approaches—an intermediate zone, potentially in close cultural contact with Ireland and South Wales on the one hand, and on the other, Britanny, Gaul and the Mediterranean beyond. It is demonstrable that cultural and economic intercourse along these western seaways is particularly in evidence during those periods when the eastern zone is subject to invasion from the Continent. And Vortigern's employment of the Saxon fleet as mercenaries implied that the Roman Channel Fleet no longer offered protection to the crossing of the narrow seas. Paradoxically, the *Adventus Saxonum* which severed Lowland Britain from its traditional European contacts, actually created the conditions for a cultural Golden Age further west.

The end of the Roman period in the West Country is characterised by the re-occupation of ancient British defended sites—perhaps a native parallel to the sophisticates' flight to the fortified towns. As in the Roman province of Germania Superior, where the fourth century witnessed a similar re-occupation of pre-Roman hilltop strongholds, this seems to represent an entirely native and un-Roman response to the Germanic threat from across the *limes*. Possibly the pre-Roman tradition had been unbroken in some places. There is evidence to suggest that one or two sites in the further west, such as the promontory-fort at Trevelgue Head, may never have been abandoned. And as in Germania Superior, some such hillforts—like that at High Peak, near Sidmouth on the Devon coast—seem to have been entirely new, rather than refurbished fortifications. Most, like Chun Castle and Castle Dore in Cornwall, were simple circular forts of a south-western Iron Age type where the defences required little if any modification. Small and easily defended, these seem clearly to reflect the comitatus society of the nascent 'Heroic Age'. The fortress of Cadbury-Camelot, on the other hand, lying at the eastern edge of the region in south Somerset, was very much more formidable. Strongly refortified and enclosing in all some 18 acres, it implies the existence of powerful regional government during at least part of the post-Roman phase. Possibly this phase also saw the construction of large linear earthworks of the kind which in late Roman times were thrown up to defend the more important estates against external attack—and which are particularly widespread and numerous in the west. The rock-cut ditch and embankment of Bokerly Dyke, originally conceived to defend an imperial estate in north Dorset in the fourth century, continued to be refurbished into the fifth. And perhaps earthworks like Bolster Bank near St Agnes Head on the north Cornwall coast, or the Giant's Hedge extending east of Castle Dore, represent merely local boundary works serving to enclose the home estate of a local chieftain. On a larger scale, however, the massive embankment of West Wansdyke, lying between Maes Knoll and Selwood, and clearly protecting the south-west from incursions from the Avon Valley and the Cotswolds beyond (so soon to come into Saxon hands) would seem to imply a very much more concerted administrative organisation.

The new hilltop defences almost certainly represent the strongholds of a local military or political elite. The replacement of the Roman bureaucracy by petty kings or *tyranni* dominating relatively small areas, probably reflects an unconscious reversion to the ancient pre-Roman units of territory, determined as much by the minutiae of local economies and physical geography as by larger loyalties. Each fort would dominate its immediate vicinity, the local native population sharing both in its protection and its economic organisation. And in the face of social and political instability due as much to internal unrest as to external pressure, no doubt such forts might serve not only to defend the local population against external attack, but also to ensure in case of need the personal protection of the *tyrannus* and his retinue from their 'subjects'. But if the occasion of this development is clear: the simultaneous *Adventus Saxonum* in the east and the persistence of seaborne Irish raiding parties in the west, the exact origins of those who set themselves up as local *tyranni* are shrouded in mystery. They may have come from the last of the 'Roman' aristocracy—perhaps from among those rich landowners, now the urban nobility. Or they may represent a quite new ruling class, rising Spartacus-like from the ranks of the peasantry—former native bailiffs perhaps, or even estate labourers. Or, not impossibly, they may have been noblemen from further east, or immigrant Irish or Welsh, or even Picts, incomers from outside the region, taking advantage of the final collapse of the Roman administration to seize lands and power. But whatever the circumstances, this development was to initiate the phase of crisis and reaction to the barbarian invasion which was to culminate in victory for the West at Mount Badon *c*.500 and usher in that Golden Age whose decline Gildas would lament less than fifty years later.

Whatever may have been the reputed character of these early patrons of the Golden Age—like the impious sixth-century overlord of the south-west, Constantine, whom Gildas was to berate as 'tyrannical whelp of the unclean lioness of Dumnonia', the most important single factor during these post-Roman centuries was the spread of Christianity. Although there is some evidence that the late Roman native Church survived in the urban centres, the ancient pre-Christian religions revived, and even flourished, especially among the *pagani* of the countryside. The new Christianity we meet with now was intrusive, distinctive and monastic in character. It happened that the renewed activity along the western seaways in post-Roman times coincided with the great monastic movement which, emanating ultimately from the east Mediterranean, was to spread via south Gaul to the entire Atlantic seaboard, including especially at this time the Welsh coastal plain and Ireland. And it was this movement which was to give the Golden Age of Gildas its distinctive character as 'the Age of Saints'. The earliest definable area of this post-Roman Christianity in the south-west lies in a belt running eastwards from the Camel estuary through north-east Cornwall and into south-west Devon. Here there are found traces of a number of monastic settlements, one of which on the headland at Tintagel has been explored. The indications of parochial dedications, together with memorial stones using ogham script, or with Irish names in Roman lettering, support the quasi-historical suggestions embodied in early saints' *Lives* that this development was brought by Irish settlers coming, at least in part, via South Wales rather than from Ireland direct, during the later fifth century. The presence of intrusive grass-marked pottery also shows the Irish connection with the furthest western part of the peninsula.

The monastic mission seems to have been carried out for the most part by saints like Petroc, Sampson or Juliot—*peregrini pro amore deo*, employing the western seaways, coming commonly from south Wales, entering the south-western peninsula by one of the north-coast estuaries that provided the most obvious points of entry to the interior, crossing by way of one of the transpeninsular routes, and in due course typically passing on into Britanny. The *Life* of the early sixth-century saint Sampson offers a particularly graphic picture of conditions in the south-western peninsula at this time. Written early in the seventh century, the *Life of St Sampson* represents, together with the tracts by Gildas, the only really reliable historical works from this era. Born *c*.486, Sampson was educated at Llantwit in Glamorgan and in due course was ordained priest and bishop. In about 521 he sailed for Cornwall, apparently landing in the Camel estuary, the traditional point of entry on the north coast. In the wooded coastal area to the north he found small monastic settlements. After consulting with some of the monks he met there, and arranging for a cart to convey his holy vessels and books, he passed on into the high, inhospitable, moorland interior. In the region of Trigg he encountered barbaric pagan practices, preached successfully to the native population, and left a cross-pecked monument of the kind characteristic of the Celtic Church, before proceeding to the settlements on the south coast. There he lived for a time as a hermit in a cave by a river, and gave orders for the foundation of a monastery nearby—presumably St Sampson's in Golant (see p. 32). And in due course he embarked for Britanny and wider fame.

11

The monasteries founded by these saints were, for the most part, small communities, responsible for the conversion and pastoral care of the surrounding districts. An enclosure—the *vallum monasterii*—served to mark the separation of the community from the secular world. Within the enclosure lay the church, the dwellings of the monks and the other buildings for their pastoral and secular life. A few, like Bodmin, were larger, with monastic schools, libraries etc. Such centres formed a natural meeting place for traders and others. But the Celtic Church never forgot its oriental inspiration. The supreme good was the life of the hermit, the solitary who sought salvation in the desert. One such settlement has been explored on the little island of St Helen in the Scillies.

Both the re-occupied princely strongholds and the new monastic settlements are characterised by imported types of pottery of the later fifth and sixth century. This pottery is significant not simply for the chronological evidence it furnishes as to the occupation of these sites, but also for what it implies about the manner of life of the people concerned and the extent of their international trade and cultural connections. Four major varieties of intrusive, imported pottery occur, all wheel-made. Two classes of vessels were imported from the Mediterranean from the 460s and 70s when the western Mediterranean was once more free of Vandal pirates. There was fine red table-ware: dishes and bowls made in northern Tunisia and around the Dardanelles in the late Roman tradition (Class A). Frequently stamped on the interior with a cross symbol, this sort of vessel would not have been unsuitable for ritual purposes, and where found on monastic sites may well have served some liturgical function. And there was a large range of amphorae from the East Mediterranean, in red, pink or cream fabric, often decorated with corrugations (Class B). Such large containers were probably not imported for their own sake, but for their contents: wine, oil and possibly dry goods like raisins. This might indicate the tastes of an aristocratic society accustomed to Roman luxuries—although oil and wine would also have been important adjuncts to religious ritual. Nearer home from Aquitaine came a distinctive type of grey bowls and mortaria with a blue-black wash perhaps intended to resemble silver or pewter (Class D). A fourth class of hard, but rougher-looking kitchen ware: cooking-pots, pitchers and so forth, apparently came from the same area, continuing into a rather later date in the sixth and seventh centuries (Class E). It seems improbable that this pottery should come in ships by itself; Mediterranean glassware was not unknown, and by the same

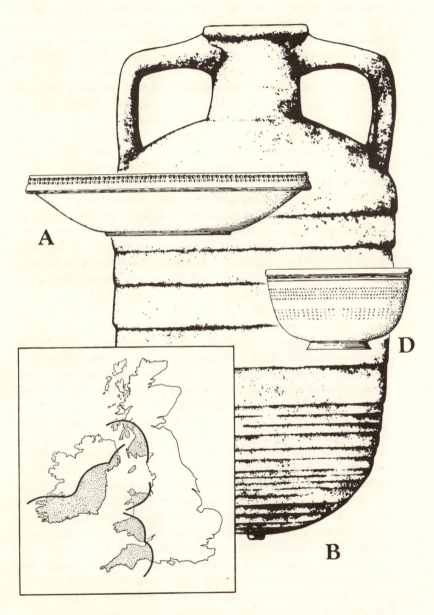

Figure 1   Reconstructions of imported pottery types A, B and D (scale ¼) and
(inset) schematised map of their distribution in the British Isles.

token, silks, spices and other exotic and perishable imports may well have been brought to coastal trading-sites like those at Bantham and Mothecombe on the south Devon coast. As Leontius' *Life of St John the Almoner* suggests, in the absence of a monetary economy, such expensive long-distance imports will have been paid for either by gold and silver bullion, or by local products such as: lead, tin, wolf-hounds or slaves, or perhaps more ordinary rural produce: cheese, leather and wool. In any case, such a trading economy implies a relatively peaceful and stable society in the south-west at this time.

But the British revival which followed the check to Saxon political and military expansion after the victory at Mount Badon, *c*.500, would last for little more than half a century. The British were entering one of those twilight periods which occur at the end of civilisations and which (as with the Geats in contemporary Sweden, where the great figure of Beowulf was to arise), promote the emergence of national heroes, whose true character is distorted by the half-light in which they move. But for whatever reason—whether renewed external attack, or the internal civil conflicts alluded to by Gildas and reflected in the later romances of *Morte d'Arthur*—any political or economic cohesion which had survived from late Roman times into the heroic age of petty princelings could not lead to effective resistance to West Saxon pressure when the time came. Such evidence as we have suggests that the defences of the princely strongholds of the south-west were falling into disrepair in the later sixth century; and the lack of material finds attributable to this period suggests that they may simply have been abandoned; there is no evidence for their violent destruction, although High Peak, at least, seems to have ended by fire.

After the battle of Deorham in 577, the Cotswolds and the lower Severn Basin were firmly in Saxon hands. But control of the south-western peninsula was not easily achieved. A major onslaught began with the seventh century. Exeter was safely in English hands by the middle years of the century; and by the 680s, when Boniface attended the English-style monastery school there, the battle-front had already moved further to the west. In 682 the Anglo-Saxon Chronicle asserts that the West Saxon king Centwine 'drove the Britons as far as the sea'. At the same time, the Atlantic sea routes which for centuries had formed the life-line of the western provinces were compromised. The Arab conquest of Spain and southern Gaul in the late seventh and early eighth centuries must to some extent have disrupted the maritime economy. And as the command of the sea passed into the control of

Islam, the old Mediterranean connection which had served the Celtic west so well for so long was at last broken. Simultaneously we hear of the renewed penetration of Saxon influence in Scotland and Ireland. Even then, the further peninsula retained some degree of independence. During the ninth century the British of the south-west were clearly felt to be a continuing threat—ever ready to join the Viking army against a common enemy. The religious and political conquest was largely consolidated by Athelstan in the early tenth century.

It is against this background of national identity under threat that the local Arthurian concern must be seen. Already by the early twelfth century the Arthurian legend was firmly lodged in popular lore and toponymy. Travelling westwards from Exeter in 1113, a group of canons from Laon entered what they were told was *terra Arturi* and were shown 'Arthur's Chair' and 'Arthur's Oven'. Later at Bodmin they became involved in a street-brawl, avoiding bloodshed only with difficulty, as a result of one of their attendant's scepticism at the notion that Arthur still lived. The fact that bloodshed was avoided only with difficulty on this occasion, is significant. It was not without some political consequence that regal pressure was brought to bear on the monks of Glastonbury to search for Arthur's grave—the discovery of which was finally reported in 1190. Thereafter the proliferation of actual 'relics' merely paralleled the development of the romance legends.

II

TINTAGEL

THE EXPOSED, cliff-girt headland of Tintagel lies on the northern coast of Cornwall, projecting over a quarter of a mile into the Atlantic and rising 250 feet above the waves. Now practically an island, the headland is separated from the mainland by a natural cleft, spanned only by a low and continually crumbling isthmus. This seems to have been a development largely of the thirteenth and fourteenth centuries. In the early twelfth century Geoffrey of Monmouth could describe the access as 'so narrow that three armed knights might hold it against the entire realm of Britain'. In any case, the original appearance of this part is now disguised by the later medieval fortification. In earlier times a broader neck of land joined the promontory to the mainland. At its landward end the headland was cut off by a bluff of rock, now scarped, and the *vallum monasterii:* a rampart composed of an earthen bank eight feet high and a broad, flat-bottomed ditch, 25 feet across—now crowned by the thirteenth-century castle curtain wall.

On this remote headland a monastery was founded in the fifth century, probably by the principal missionary of the area, St Julian or Juliot, one of the sons of Brychan, a south Welsh king of the fifth century. Here he built his cell, and probably a simple church or oratory. And soon attracting others, a flourishing monastic community was established. There seem to have been some three or four building periods before the site was abandoned. The Anglo-French name Tintagel came only with the castle erected by the Earls of Cornwall in the twelfth and thirteenth centuries. The original name of the place is unknown. But it is possible that it may have been Rosnant, referred to in several Irish sources. The precise etymology of Rosnant is uncertain, but arguably it meant 'Headland by the Valley',.which very adequately describes the Tintagel location. If this was the Rosnant of Irish tradition, then it was here that such early saints as Enda and Tighernach received their education, in the school presided over by Maucannus, or Mawgan. Within the vallum here the monks lived in small contiguous cells, with rough stone walls set in clay, trodden earth floors and thatched roofs. The cells are rectangular in plan, rather than in the circular-hut tradition found in the majority of British and Irish monasteries, which suggests a Continental or Mediterranean prototype. Eight such clusters of buildings have been located and explored—two of them largely destroyed by the later castle builders. Some lay on the relatively level surface of the headland; others huddled along natural folds and artificial terraces cut into the more sheltered eastern cliff-slopes of the island. Both the vallum and monastic buildings were dated by fragments of imported Mediterranean pottery indicating a foundation some time in the later fifth century. And these cells, together with other communal buildings, may have housed anything between thirty and hundred monks in all.

Site A. There can be little doubt that the main complex, of some dozen or more small rooms, clusters round the later castle chapel, which no doubt replaced the original monastic church. A rectangular building 48 x 16 feet running beneath the western end of the chapel, and constructed with masonry courses set obliquely, in a style quite different from anything else at Tintagel, may well represent all that remains of Juliot's original settlement. To the south of the medieval chapel lies the base of a tomb-shrine or *leacht* of a type well-known in Ireland, five feet square and originally perhaps three feet high, used to contain relics. A foundation of unusual solidarity alongside this *leacht* may represent the remains of a small church or oratory. Four shallow, rock-cut graves located to the north of the medieval chapel were possibly those of more important members of the community. Probably a large cemetery remains to be discovered on the headland. Fragments of a small slate slab found among the debris of the chapel may represent the frontal of a stone altar. The complex of buildings that developed round this original nucleus presumably served for the reception and lodging of pilgrims who came to visit the shrine.

These buildings were relatively easily reached from the mainland. But those situated on the cliff terraces were accessible only by steep paths or rock-cut stairways leading down from the plateau. And it is these sites which seem to have been more intimately connected with the inner life of the monastery. Although the plan and character of these buildings are often obscured by successive phases of modification and rebuilding, it is possible at least tentatively to identify their various functions in the monastic life.

Immediately beyond the medieval castle lies *Site F,* built on two artificial terraces cut into the cliff-side. A single room on the upper

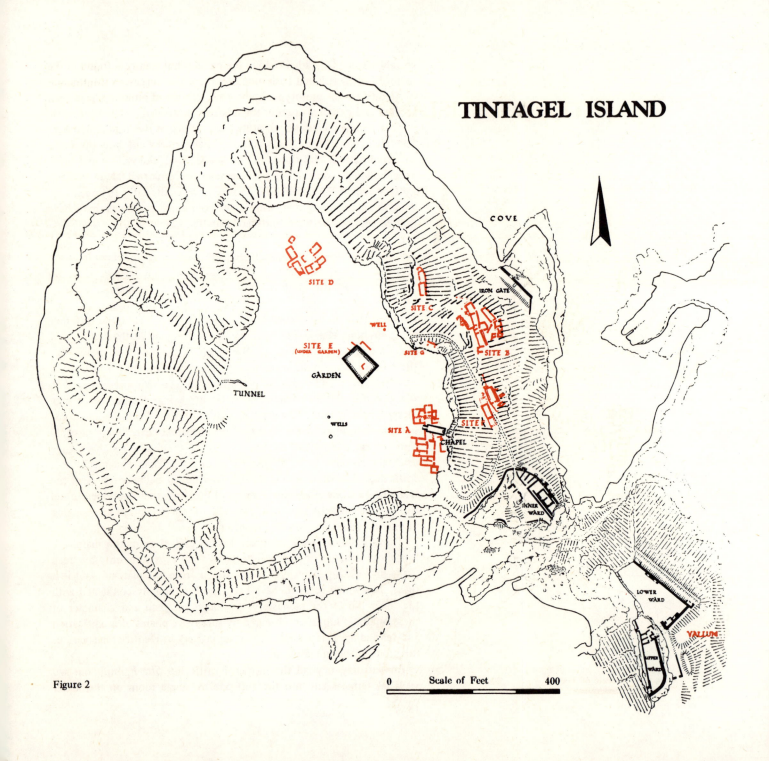

TINTAGEL ISLAND

COVE

SITE D

IRON GATE

SITE C

WELL

SITE E
(UNDER GARDEN)

SITE G

SITE B

GARDEN

TUNNEL

WELLS

SITE A

SITE F

CHAPEL

INNER
WARD

LOWER
WARD

VALLUM

UPPER
WARD

Figure 2

0   Scale of Feet   400

terrace had channels, partly rock-cut, below the floor, possibly for heating. The lower terrace had a long room, originally with doors at each end. On the upper side a heavy stone base, with slots for wooden uprights, indicated the former existence of heavy cupboards or presses. On the lower side two doors led to small open-ended annexes, which would have afforded a better light and could have served for studies or scriptoria, especially in fair weather; they recall the story of St Columba, sitting at the door of his hut (*tegoriolum*) copying the Scriptures. It may be suggested that the complex on Site F constituted the library, school and scriptorium of the community.

Further to the north, *Site B* lies lower down the cliff face: an irregular collection of buildings running down the slope and spreading onto two further artificial terraces. At the further end of the upper terrace stood a two-storied building, its gabled roof running out at right-angles from the cliff-face, in which sockets had been cut for the three horizontal beams. A large adjacent room is distinguished by an external stone bench, which would have provided a warm and sheltered place for study, looking out across the sea. Behind these buildings lay a stairway ascending the cliff and providing direct access to the church and other buildings on the plateau. At one end of the lower terrace two small

Figure 3   Tintagel: artist's reconstruction of Site B.

chambers with paved flooring crazed by heat, and found covered with wood ash, almost certainly represent sweat-houses—water being thrown onto a heated floor to provide steam baths. From the lower end of Site B a path leads down to a small rock-hewn pool, filled by the overflow from the monastic well. Further down the cliff still, a steep path leads through the 'iron gate' of the thirteenth-century curtain wall and through a cleft in the rocks to a small cove; sheltered from the prevailing westerly winds, this no doubt served as an ancient landing-place. Other buildings at *Sites C and G* nearby suggest that this whole cliff-side complex formed one of the major living-quarters in the monastery—which, perhaps with a communal hall or refectory serving this group of buildings, might have housed between, say, twenty and thirty members of the community. A further terrace roughly quarried on the cliff above Site C was never occupied by buildings, but the soil revealed traces of cultivation and the space was probably employed as a garden.

The water supply flowing down the cliff between these various groups of cells came from a well lying on the plateau between the later castle garden and the edge of the cliff. A shallow spring-fed basin, this is covered by a small well-chamber provided with narrow rock-cut steps leading down to the water, and a corbelled roof to prevent pollution.

To the north of the plateau but sheltered on the lee-side of a rock outcrop lay a further group of buildings, *Site D*. Poorly constructed by comparison with other buildings on the island, and with little sign of human occupation, it is probable that this complex represents the centre of the monastery's agricultural activities; certainly one room contains a kiln of the type used at this period for drying corn. This in itself possibly suggests inland cultivation. Evidence of further buildings in and around the site of the castle garden was found, *Site E*, but no coherent plan was recovered.

The later stages of the monastic occupation at Tintagel are marked by a progressive degeneration in building technique. There is no evidence to suggest that the community came to a violent end. Probably the site was simply abandoned due to social and economic factors consequent upon the decay and final loss of the Mediterranean connections. Nothing on the site suggests a date later than the eighth century. The remaining monks may have once more taken to the life of *peregrini*, or may simply have moved *en bloc* to a more viable community like that of St Petroc's at Bodmin, into whose hands ownership of the site had come before the time of the Domesday survey in 1086.

Figure 4   Tintagel: designs from stone trial pieces (scale $^1/_3$).

Naturally defensible, the site was fortified in the twelfth century by Reginald de Dunstanville, an illegitimate son of Henry I, who was created Earl of Cornwall in 1141. The original name of the Celtic settlement was no doubt lost in the interim, and an appropriate Anglo-Norman name was supplied. (cf. the name of a rocky headland on the island of Sark called Tintageu, earlier Tente d'Agel, interpreted in the local patois as 'The Castle of the Devil'.) Of the twelfth-century castle only the chapel-nave and remains of the Great Hall survive. In 1236 the castle was acquired by Earl Richard, the younger brother of Henry III, and King of the Romans from 1257. Earl Richard held Tintagel until 1272, and carried through a massive refortification. Most of what can be seen today, including the curtain wall and the chapel chancel belongs to this date. In addition to the chapel, the island also contained a medieval well and a small rectangular walled garden; nearby, the hummocky surface marks the site of a man-made rabbit-warren.

The castle was never residential, although in the late fourteenth century it was used for the incarceration of state prisoners. The severance of the island, as a result of erosion, took place about 1300. In the fourteenth century the gap was spanned by a bridge, but even this had disappeared before 1500. By the sixteenth century the gap between the mainland and the island had widened almost to its present proportions, and the site was derelict. The island, reached only by a dangerous scramble across the broken neck of the peninsula, was abandoned to sheep and rabbits. In 1584 the surveyor John Norden described the passage to the island as now made:

> farr more irksome and trowblesome by a little isthmos or neck of lande which lyeth at the foote of the rock of ilande, the descent unto it verie steepe and craggie, from whence the ascente againe is farr more tedious and daungerous, by a verie narrow, rockye, and wyndinge waye up the steepe sea-clyffe, under which the sea waves wallow, and so assayle the foundation of the Ile, as may astonish an unstable brayne to consider the perill, for the leaste slipp of the foote sendes the whole bodye into the devouringe sea. . . . He must have his eyes that will scale Tyntagell.

The earliest connection between the castle of Tintagel and King Arthur occurs in Geoffrey of Monmouth's *Historia Regum Britanniae*, written in the middle years of the twelfth century. In this, Tintagel appears as the fortress of Gorlois, Duke of Cornwall, and the scene of Ygraine's seduction by Uther, after his entry into the fortress has been contrived by Merlin's magic aid; and by implication Tintagel is the birthplace of Arthur. The same story of Arthur's birth is repeated shortly

Figure 5 Sketch of Tintagel from John Norden's *Description of Cornwall*, 1584.

afterwards in the late twelfth-century French *Romance of Merlin*. Geoffrey's vivid description indicates that he knew the site; and it may not be insignificant that he wrote his *Historia* at the time when the first castle on the island was under construction. Excavation shows that the Norman builders must have uncovered at least part of the earlier monastic remains; and no doubt romance imagination supplied the connection: if this was the site of the residence of the Norman Earls of Cornwall, then here was tangible proof of their predecessor Duke Gorlois' palace.

Apart from the episode of Arthur's conception and birth, Tintagel does not otherwise play a large part in Arthurian romance. But of particular interest for the light it throws on romance-writers' use of local topography, is the thirteenth-century Grail romance *Perceval li Gallois*. In this, Arthur comes to Tintagel with Lancelot and Gawain, and finds that the enclosure of the castle has fallen into an abyss, so that it is unapproachable on that side. But a fine gateway remains. They enter, to find an ancient great hall and beyond it a beautiful chapel. There an old priest reveals to the king the story of his birth, adding that it was by reason of the sinful circumstances of his conception that the headland was even then being engulfed. In another series of romances

23

Tintagel figures more prominently—but as the castle of King Mark (and the scene of Tristan and Iseult's liaison), arbitrarily transferred from the south coast of Cornwall. To the romance mind certainly, Tintagel must have seemed a more appropriately regal location for an ancient ruler of Cornwall than the little-known site of Lancien (see p. 32).

The romantic scenery and its connection with the medieval Arthurian cycle brought renewed fame to Tintagel in the nineteenth century when literary interest in Arthurian romance revived. The work of the local poet R. S. Hawker, vicar of Morwenstow, and more importantly Tennyson's *Idylls of the King*, popularised the story; and the site was all that could be desired. The revival of interest is marked by the making of a new path up to the island, and the repair of the castle ruins in 1852. The London and South-Western Railway brought Tintagel within reach of the tourist, and the massive King Arthur Hotel (originally distinguished by a series of mural paintings depicting Arthurian scenes—now unfortunately obliterated—and a Waring and Gillow reproduction of the Winchester 'Round Table') was built on the cliff edge dominating the landscape. A host of mid-Victorian visitors have left us graphic verbal pictures of Tintagel—some avowedly 'unsentimental', others inevitably caught up in the sheer romanticism of the scene. Typical is that by Mrs H. Craik, author of *John Halifax Gentleman* and an Arthurian 'sceptic', who wrote:

> Nothing small, or cowardly, or luxurious, nothing after the pattern of Regent Street loungers, or Pall Mall club-ites could possibly exist here, on this wild inaccessible rock, facing, day and night, summer and winter, that awful lonely sea. No man could voluntarily make his dwelling here without being daring, self-contained, prudent and strong—qualities exacted by the very necessities of his life. And no woman—call her Guinevere, Ysolte, anything—could sit here on this rock, with this sublime desolation around her, without feeling strange thoughts come unto her, strange passions tear her, strange experiences teach her. . . . Surely the men who lived here, and the women who belonged to them, could not have been ordinary men and women.

But the tourist wave has destroyed at least the environs of this romantic scene. Already in mid-Victorian times the village was described by another visitor, Dr Henry Alford, Dean of Canterbury, as 'surely one of the dreariest in Europe'. And it has since degenerated to what Professor Thomas rightly calls 'a distasteful straggle of knick-knack shops and spurious Arthurian peepshows'.

III

CASTLE DORE AND THE TRISTAN STONE

THIRTY MILES south of Tintagel on the opposite side of Cornwall, Castle Dore lies on the back of a low ridge, bounded on the east by the tidal estuary of the Fowey, and on the west by a wide marshy valley which extends inland beyond Tywardreath ('the house on the strand'), its etymology indicating that in former times the sea extended well inland of the present coastline. The site lies on the lee side of the ridge, ensuring some degree of protection from the prevailing westerly winds, while still affording extensive views towards the sea. Along this ridge ran the ancient transpeninsular trackway which linked the southern harbours with those on and around the estuary of the Camel on the north coast—the traditional points of entry and departure. Passing through Bodmin, the site of an important Celtic monastery and the seat of a ninth-century Celtic bishop, this route was marked by a series of standing stone crosses—those which survive dating from the ninth to the eleventh centuries.

A simple defensive enclosure of the smaller pre-Roman type of southwestern fort, Castle Dore has two roughly circular ramparts, contiguous on the west and gradually diverging towards the east so as to form a barbican affording protection to the entrance. The outer rampart consists of an earthen bank 35-40 feet across and about 6 feet high, surrounded by a ditch 22 feet wide and originally 12 feet deep, although now silted up to a mere 4 feet. The inner rampart was similar, although the bank was rather narrower—24 feet across and rising to about 7 feet. Some 250 feet in diameter, this inner rampart encloses an area of almost an acre. The present gap in the defences to the east, and the rounded ends of the banks, is due to ploughing. Originally the entrances were very much narrower—perhaps only some 6 feet wide— and contained wood-lined tunnels passing beneath a bridge linking the rampart footwalk on either side above. A ditch-lined roadway seems to have crossed the barbican area linking inner and outer gateways. Early descriptions of the site record an outwork, consisting of a bank and ditch, beyond the outer gate, which may have been used for stabling

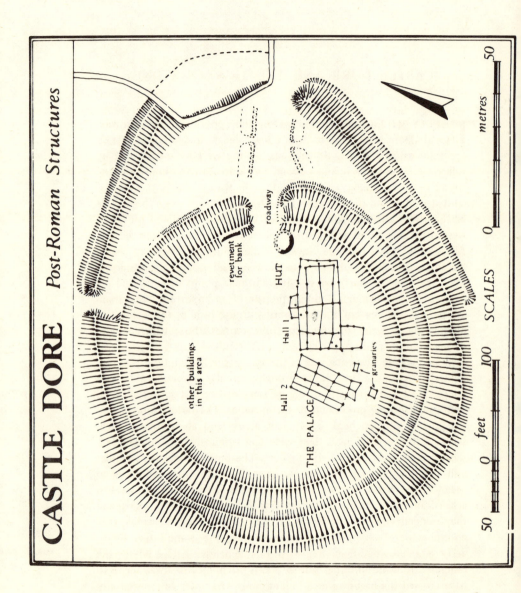

CASTLE DORE
Post-Roman Structures

other buildings in this area

revetment for bank

roadway

HUT

Hall 1

Hall 2

granaries

THE PALACE

SCALES

metres 50 · · · · 0

feet 50 · · · · 0 · · · 100

Figure 6

or as a cattle enclosure, or possibly even for cultivation; but this is no longer discernible.

The site seems to have been abandoned some time late in the first century A.D., presumably as a result of the Roman advance. And then after an hiatus of some four centuries, the fort was reoccupied in post-Roman times, and its defences refurbished—the fallen bank strengthened with a dry-stone revetment, and apparently built up to provide a level fighting-platform. Intensive ploughing has destroyed most floor levels together with the usual debris associated with occupation. But the main outlines of this post-Roman phase are clear on stratigraphical evidence. The entrance was provided with a roughly cobbled roadway about 6 feet in width, lying on top of some 2 feet of fallen rubbish from the pre-Roman gate. On the south side, within the gate, was a small oval hut, probably with wattled walls on a stone base and a paved floor. It was probably some sort of guardhouse or porter's lodge of the kind mentioned in early Welsh laws and in romances such as *Culhwch and Olwen*. The outer gate was not investigated, but must have been defensible, and possibly was provided with the same sort of gateway postulated at Cadbury-Camelot (see pp. 53, 56).

However, the major feature of the interior at this date was the erection of at least two large timber halls. Both buildings were constructed on the same principles, with stone-lined postholes containing roughly squared timbers about a foot across. Hall 1 was an aisled structure of four bays, about 90 feet long and 40 feet wide. It must have supported a pitched roof, not impossibly with some sort of clerestory in the Roman basilican style. It had a central hearth, and was entered by a small porch at the centre of the long north side. The aisle returned along the eastern end of the hall, and presumably represents some sort of domestic passage. Curtains, or perhaps light wooden partitions of some kind might have divided the interior. A secondary structure, roughly 24 feet square, projected from the south-western corner of the hall, perhaps with its own gable set at right-angles to that of the main roof. This annexe might be interpreted as a bower. Hall 2 lay at a little space from the first, and at an angle to it. Merely 65 x 35 feet in plan, this seems to have been a somewhat simpler building, of only three bays; but it has the same rectangular annexe lying at one corner. What may have been a third hall of this type, with a roughly cobbled floor, was located in the northern part of the interior; but this sector was not fully explored and no coherent plan was recovered.

Two small rectangular buildings, about 7 x 5 feet, lay to the south of

Hall 2. Although small, these were constructed with substantial posts and were clearly intended to bear some weight. It is possible that they represent the foundations of bell- or watch-towers; but more probably they should be identified with granaries of a well-known early type, raised on posts to keep the grain dry. The northern quadrant of the interior was scarcely touched, and the western not at all, so further buildings probably remain to be discovered in this area, while no doubt outhouses of some kind lay within the outside enclosure. But although much of the site remains unexcavated, sufficient was discovered for us to recognise a pattern of buildings which fits well into the traditional picture of the court of a Celtic king as defined in medieval Welsh and Irish law texts. The Dimetian Code, for example, listed nine buildings which the king's tenants were obliged to erect within his *dun*: a hall, chamber, kitchen, chapel, barn, kiln-house, stable, dog-kennel and privy. The proportions of a king's hall as described in the ninth-century *Crith Gablach* are very much those of the smaller of these two halls. And although Castle Dore had defences that were already extant, it is note-worthy that the 250 feet diameter of the interior compares favourably with the standard laid down in the *Crith Gablach*, which states that the king's *dun* should measure seven-score feet every way, with a rampart tapering from 12 feet thick at the bottom to 7 feet at the top, and surrounded by a 12 foot ditch.

Figure 7   Castle Dore: artist's reconstruction of palace complex.

The destruction of the occupation-levels, and the failure to locate any associated midden area, means that secure dating evidence for the post-Roman phase is slight—represented merely by a handful of beads and two fragments of pottery which can be matched at Gwithian, where parallels were ascribed to the sixth century. The outside limits of occu-

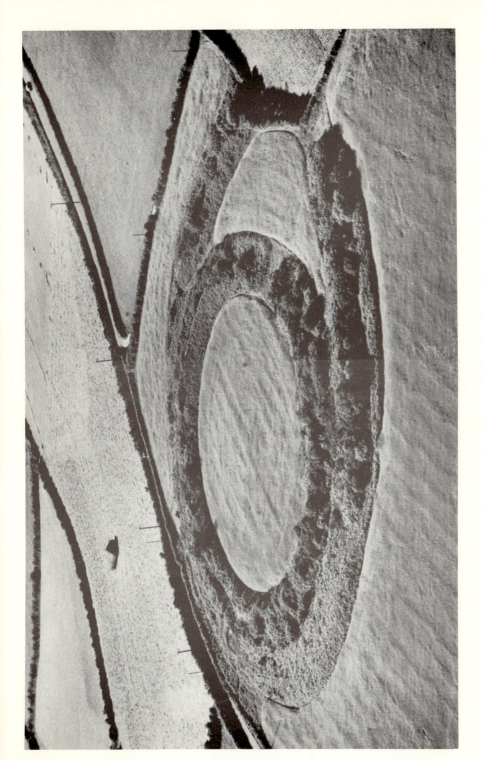

Plate I   Castle Dore: aerial view from the south.

Plate II   The Tristan Stone

pation probably lie between the fifth and eighth centuries; certainly the fort is unlikely to have survived the Saxon domination of this region in the ninth or early tenth century. By the twelfth century the site served as a quarry; and although its character was not forgotten, William of Worcester who saw it in 1478 spoke of it as 'ruined'.

Castle Dore is perfectly in accordance with the traditional picture of a Celtic chieftain's palace, occupying a strategic position controlling the important transpeninsular route; here, if anywhere, we might expect to find the seat of the chieftain who ruled south Cornwall in early medieval times. And on the other side of the Fowey estuary the Giant's Hedge, running between the rivers Lerryn and Looe and enclosing an area of some twenty miles, could well represent the boundary of the home estate or demesne dependent on that seat.

An inscribed stone, datable to the first half of the sixth century, and originally recorded as standing a short distance south of Castle Dore, gives a clue to one of the owners. The words DRUSTANUS HIC IACIT | CUNOMORI FILIUS, 'Here lies Drustanus, son of Cunomorus', are cut in two lines running vertically down one face of the stone. Cunomorus, or to use a more modern form, Cynfawr, is the name of a known king of Dumnonia, the predecessor and probably the father of Constantine—the ruler denounced by Gildas. Constantine was an old man in 540 and a memorial to a brother would accord well with the date of the stone. The name Drustanus is philologically identical with Tristan, the hero of one of the most popular medieval romances, *Tristan and Iseult*. In this connection it is significant that the *Life* of the sixth-century saint, Paul Aurelian, written in 880 by Wrmonoc, a monk of Landevennec in Britanny, states that a certain Marcus, king of what may be assumed to be Cornwall at this date, was also known by the alternative name of Cunomorus (*quem alio nomine Quonomorium vocant*). Now the coincidence between a Tristan, son of Marcus *alias* Cunomorus, and the famous Tristan, nephew of King Mark of Cornwall, is remarkable. Although no surviving version of the romance makes Tristan the son rather than the nephew of Mark, it is not impossible that this should have been the original version, later altered as a matter of courtly propriety.

In the middle of the sixth century burial in a consecrated cemetery was becoming usual, but had not yet entirely supplanted the older custom of burial in a family graveyard. It was customary to set up memorial stones in isolation, and often on the road-side in the Roman manner; and it would not be unreasonable to suppose that this stone

31

marked the site of an aristocratic burial alongside the road leading to his residence, in the fashion of Roman aristocracy.

The oldest surviving version of the *Tristan and Iseult* romance is contained in a poem by the Anglo-Norman, Beroul, who places King Mark's 'lofty palace' at Lancien. The celebrated Celticist, Professor Loth, identified Lancien with Lantyan (Domesday Book Lantien), now a farm rather over a mile north of Castle Dore, but formerly the centre of one of the great Cornish medieval landholdings. Nearby, about a mile east of Castle Dore, is the church of St Sampson in Golant, which could well represent the monastery of St Sanson, to which Iseult went by a paved road and to which she gave a gold-embroidered robe, converted into a chasuble and still used in the time of Beroul, or of the source from which he drew. Loth postulates other, less certain, identifications. Rather further afield in south Cornwall, for instance, Beroul's Morrois, the forest in which the lovers hid from King Mark, may possibly have lain in the neighbourhood of the manor of Moresc; the Evil Ford, *le Mal Pas*, may be represented in the present river-crossing at Malpas, south of Truro; and it is not impossible that *La Blanche Lande* might have been a straightforward translation of the name of the manor of Tir Gwyn, the slopes of which are still strewn with white quartz. Not very far away in the parish of St Keverne, a land charter of 967 includes the place-name *Hryt Eselt*, the 'Ford of Iseult'.

There is little enough in the poet's conventional description of Lancien to localize the story, although a hilltop site and an earthwork like Castle Dore is a more likely site than that of the medieval manor of Lantyan set in a deep valley. The monastery of St Sampson is more significant. Only two Cornish churches are named after this saint. That at Southhill on the edge of the moors, where the church still preserves an early inscribed stone, must be connected with the earlier miracle when the saint restored a dead youth to life. The taming of the dragon, which lived in a cave by a river, and the subsequent foundation of a monastery nearby (see p. 11) point clearly to the estuary of the Fowey and the church of St Sampson in Golant, the parish in which Castle Dore lies.

But if this connection be accepted, the localisation of the story of *Tristan and Iseult* in this part of south Cornwall must go back far beyond Beroul. The Priory of St Andrew at Tywardreath was founded in the late eleventh century as a cell of the great Benedictine house of St Sergius and St Bacchus at Angers. The priory was endowed from early days with the church of Tywardreath and its dependent chapel of St Sampson in Golant. This was the position from 1100 until the early

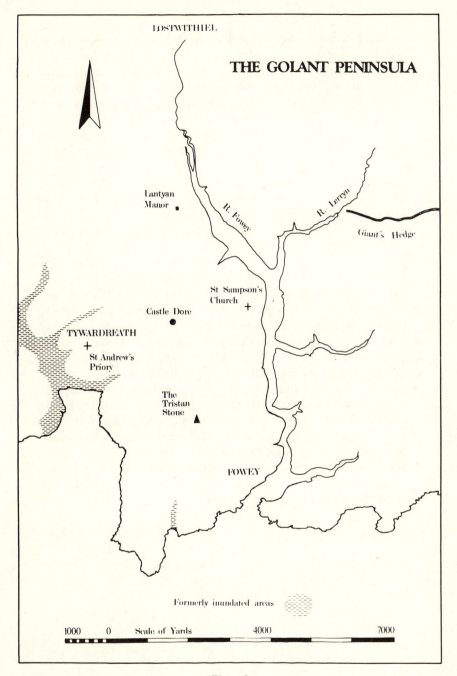

LOSTWITHIEL

THE GOLANT PENINSULA

Lantyan
Manor

R. Fowey

R. Lerryn

Giant's Hedge

St Sampson's
Church

Castle Dore

TYWARDREATH

St Andrew's
Priory

The
Tristan
Stone

FOWEY

Formerly inundated areas

1000   0   Scale of Yards   4000   7000

Figure 8

sixteenth century, when St Sampson established in independence. No one writing after the foundation of Tywardreath Priory would have taken Iseult to the 'monastery' of St Sampson or elsewhere than to the priory church. The older monastery has left no trace in the Domesday survey, and St Andrew was a favourite Saxon saint. The change in status of the two churches and the end of the monastery of St Sampson should probably be ascribed to the reorganisation of Cornwall under Athelstan in the first half of the tenth century. Whether the author of the Tristan romance was drawing on older Breton traditions, or whether the stone near the Cornish monastery of St Sampson afforded a clue on which he embroidered, must remain uncertain. But it is difficult to avoid the deduction that the romance was already localised in the Cornish-Breton milieu as early as the ninth century, and presumably in this part of south Cornwall.

The scene in the Golant peninsula may reflect more than mere topographical details. The hostility between Cornwall and the marauding Irish forms a constant theme in Beroul's romance. With archaeological evidence for the Irish lying, not in Ireland, but only some twenty miles to the north of Castle Dore at this time, it is easy to understand both the reason for the north-facing linear defence of the Giant's Hedge to protect the home demesne, and also how both hostility and marriage alliances might have been involved. The locale would provide a graphic background to the traditional Cornish-Irish antagonism, remembered and later woven into the Breton version of the Tristan story. The Breton connection may not be without significance in this respect. If Castle Dore in no sense commands mid-Cornwall, it clearly secures the southern harbours that led to Britanny. The *tyrannus* whom St Sampson aided against the Breton prince Judal was called Conmorus. It is quite conceivable that the patron of Castle Dore enjoyed some degree of power among his relatives in the Breton peninsula.

Plate III   Glastonbury: aerial view of town, abbey and tor.

Plate IV   Cadbury-Camelot: aerial view from the south; excavation in progress.

IV

GLASTONBURY

THE TOWNSHIP of Glastonbury lies on the western flank of an 'island' of land which is formed by a stone bluff rising prominently out of the Somerset Levels—an extensive region of former marshland studded with islands extending north and west to the sea. In antiquity no doubt this inundation brought navigable waters very much closer to the site. About one and a half square miles in extent, the island rises steeply to over 500 feet at the summit of the Tor, affording extensive views in all directions. To the south-east a narrow isthmus, little more than a quarter of a mile across, and rising a mere thirty feet above the former level of the marsh, links Glastonbury with the hills of East Somerset. This causeway is spanned by Ponters Ball, a linear earthwork about half a mile long, consisting of a rampart 12 feet high and 30 feet across with a 12 foot ditch on the outer side, facing east.

The island of Glastonbury has been surrounded by a plethora of legends since medieval times. And extreme, even unique, antiquity was claimed for the ecclesiastical foundation here. Writing early in the twelfth century, William of Malmesbury records that the earliest and most venerated building on the site was a structure of wattles known as the Old Church (*Vetusta Ecclesia*), which was said to have been built by disciples of missionaries who had come to Britain, sent from Rome at the request of King Lucius in the second century. This wattled structure had later been covered with wooden planks and lead in the time of Paulinus, a companion of St Augustine, in about 600. Two other churches had been built to the east of the Old Church: a second said to have been built by St David of Wales, and a third traditionally associated with twelve holy men who came from the north of Britain. Later tradition recorded a legend that the Old Church had been founded early in the Christian era by Joseph of Arimathea; while the story that it had actually been consecrated by Christ himself in honour of his Virgin mother, was already known to the anonymous tenth-century biographer of St Dunstan.

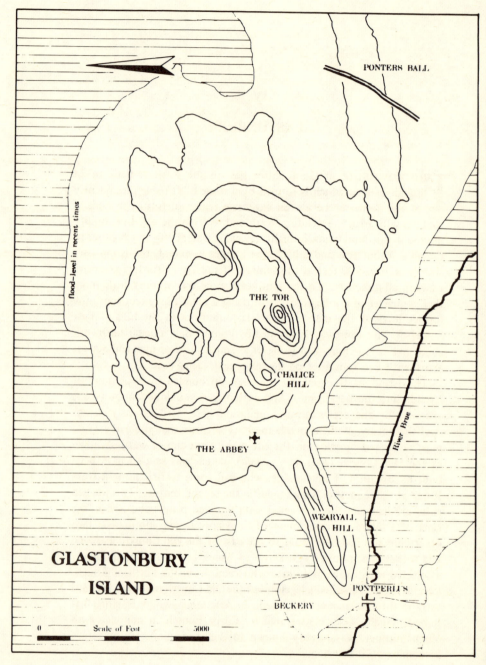

PONTERS BALL

flood-level in recent times

THE TOR

CHALICE
HILL

THE ABBEY

River Brue

WEARYALL
HILL

GLASTONBURY

ISLAND

PONTPERLUS

BECKERY

0   Scale of Feet   5000

Figure 9   Contours at 50 feet intervals.

The site was certainly such as would have appealed to the eremitical early British Church. And by the mid-sixth century, Gildas is said to have been 'charmed by the sanctity of the place'. The existence of a charter granted by an unnamed British king of Dumnonia and ascribed a date of 601 A.D. is recorded in the ancient historians who say that the local people of British descent referred to the place as Yniswitrin, by which they meant 'Glass Island', which is presumably based on a false etymology of the English name Glastonbury. Nevertheless, an early Celtic foundation is clearly probable. William of Malmesbury emphasised the Irish traditions at Glastonbury, and recorded the continuing devotion of Irish pilgrims coming to venerate the relics of early saints there. In the Church of St Mary the altar was flanked by shrines containing relics of St Patrick and of St Indracht. One life of the tenth-century Anglo-Saxon bishop Dunstan describes how he was taught by Irish teachers at Glastonbury. A further early cult with Irish connections is that of St Bridget in the chapel at Beckery, where the saint was believed to have left certain personal possessions, later preserved as relics. The etymology *Bec Eriu*, 'Little Ireland', was current at least as early as the tenth century.

Although little could be expected to have survived the disastrous fire which swept the monastery in 1184, excavation has revealed at least part of the early monastic settlement. The Celtic monastery seems to have lain beneath the western part of the later medieval layout. It was bounded to the east by the customary *vallum monasterii*, traces of which were found for a distance of about 60 yards, running roughly north-south beneath the crossing of the medieval church and again beneath the chapter house: a rampart consisting of a bank originally perhaps 25 to 30 feet across, and on its eastern side a ditch dug 25 feet across and about 10 feet deep. Although no direct dating evidence was available, the much-spread remains of the vallum were cut into by ninth-century glass furnaces which had been dug into the inner slope. The oldest remains within this vallum were those found within the ancient cemetery, the south, west and east walls of which were located; and which was apparently entered by a gate on the west. Postholes were found belonging to at least four oratories of the wattled type, although this area was so disturbed by graves and later structures that no full plan could be recovered. The best preserved was a small building 13 feet wide and over 18 feet long—the western end of which was destroyed by the later medieval cloister. Several graves were found, some of them stone-lined, and two rectangular mausolea of an early type found in Gaul, and which probably represent the original burial places for the relics of honoured founders—perhaps those of Indracht and Patrick, before their translation into the Old Church some time about the tenth century. Of the Old Church itself no trace has been found; but it could scarcely have survived the great fire of 1184, let alone the subsequent rebuilding, and then the excavation of a crypt early in the sixteenth century. However, its position is known from the twelfth-century Lady Chapel, 60 feet long by 25 feet wide, which is said to have been built on the site of its revered predecessor. There is as yet no information respecting the domestic arrangements of the Celtic monastery; probably the monks lived in huddled groups of cells similar to those at Tintagel, but built of the local wattle material.

Soon after this part of Somerset came under Saxon control, the West Saxon king Ine (688-726) had built to the east of the Old Church a new stone church in the Continental style fashionable in Kent, with nave, chancel and porticus. Perhaps from this time also, or shortly after, date the two tall stone crosses which William of Malmesbury described standing near the Old Church within or 'at the edge of' the monks' cemetery. That nearer the church stood to a height of 26 feet, and was of five stages, three of which bore panels of figural sculpture, and lettering. That further away was only 18 feet high, and of four stages; and this also bore lettering, including names which have been recognised as those of Kentwin, king of Wessex 676-85, Hedda, bishop of Winchester 677-705, and Bregored and Beorward, abbots of Glastonbury. These crosses were still erect and in place in the late fifteenth century, but were apparently pulled down at the Reformation. The earth-fast seating for one has been found some forty feet south of the Lady Chapel; the infill of the hole containing a scrap of pottery datable to about 1500. Probably the other stood a further fifteen feet to the south, marking the site of one of the two early mausolea. It is possible that in their turn these Saxon crosses had replaced simple British mono-lithic memorials of the Tristan stone type. Some time in the eighteenth century the heavily weathered remains are said to have been dragged away to form gate-posts for a local cottage.

Glastonbury assumed its final monastic character under St Dunstan, abbot from 940-57, introducing the reformed Benedictine Rule, adding to Ine's church, providing cloisters and other monastic buildings, and building a wall round the monks' cemetery so as to make 'a fair meadow, where the bodies of the saints could rest undisturbed by those who passed by'. The foundation continued to attract royal

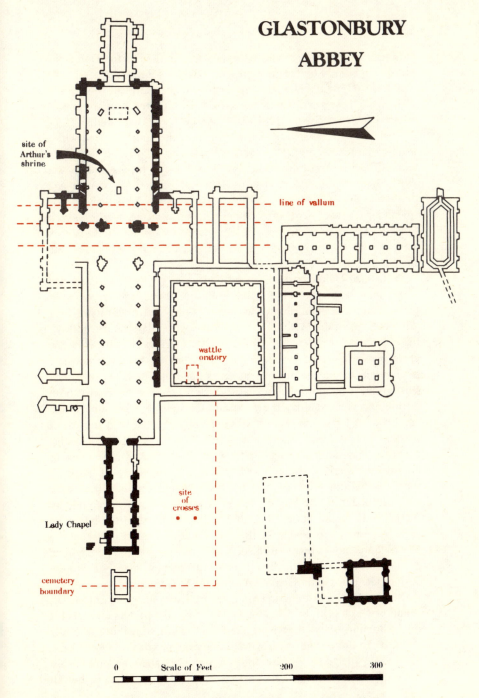

GLASTONBURY
ABBEY

site of
Arthur's
shrine

line of vallum

wattle
oratory

site
of
crosses

Lady Chapel

cemetery
boundary

0   Scale of Feet   200   300

Figure 10   Walls marked in solid black are still standing.

patronage on an even greater scale, and by the time of the Domesday survey was already by far the richest monastery in England.

But in 1184 a disastrous fire destroyed the Norman abbey, and with it all these ancient buildings. No doubt as a result of the special veneration in which the Old Church was held, the first building to be erected after the fire was a Lady Chapel on the same site, and which is now the most complete building still standing in the ruined abbey—a work of delicate late Romanesque. But although reconstruction was swift—the new quire was first used in 1213—and both church and domestic offices received addition after addition until their former splendour was surpassed, the original object of veneration—the *Vetusta Ecclesia*—was now gone, and it became necessary for the monks to seek some new object of veneration to attract pilgrims, and their money. And their search was not unsuccessful.

William of Malmesbury, a scholarly historian who seems to have had a thorough knowledge of the Glastonbury archives, and whose work gives us our most detailed knowledge of the early settlement there, himself never mentions Arthur in connection with Glastonbury. Indeed, his *History of the Kings of England* states specifically that, while the grave of Gawain is shown in Wales, 'the tomb of Arthur is nowhere to be seen, wherefore the ancient songs fable that he is yet to come'. But within little more than a century it was common belief that both Arthur and Guinevere lay buried within the abbey at Glastonbury, and the island of Glastonbury itself was explicitly equated with the Isle of Avalon, where legend said that Arthur had been taken for the healing of his wounds after his final battle with Mordred. And in the face of continuing Welsh resistance and persistent prophecies of Arthur's messianic return, proof of Arthur's death would certainly have been very acceptable to the English. Henry II was said to have been told by Welsh bards of the burial of Arthur at Glastonbury; but although he urged the monks to search for the grave, it was not until 1190 that the Glastonbury monks reported the discovery of a double grave containing the bones of an exceptionally tall man and a small woman—which were at once identified with King Arthur and Queen Guinevere.

Reports of the exhumation are given by a contemporary chronicler, Ralph of Coggeshall; by Giraldus Cambrensis, who paid a personal visit to Glastonbury shortly after the event and talked with those who had handled the bones; and by the Glastonbury monk Adam of Domerham, who wrote the history of his abbey about 1291 and who presumably drew upon archival material. These accounts differ in details, but all agree that the bodies were found deep down between the two cemetery crosses, and that they were accompanied by an inscribed leaden funerary cross. At a total depth of 16 feet, (or so it was said), was found a simple hollowed tree-trunk coffin, containing the enormous bones of a man, the skull savagely cut—some cuts knit together and one particularly deep one unhealed. Nearby, but probably separate, lay the bones of a delicate woman. Giraldus adds the circumstantial but graphic detail of a tress of golden hair which remained intact, but crumbled to dust when an over-eager monk snatched at it—falling into the hole and emerging very muddy in consequence.

About 9 feet above the coffin had been found a stone slab, on the underside of which was a leaden cross, its inscribed face against the stone. Readings of the inscription differ. Giraldus, who claimed to have handled the cross, read: HIC IACET SEPULTUS INCLITUS REX ARTHURIUS CUM WENNEVEREIA UXORE SUA SECUNDA IN INSULA AVALLONIA, 'Here lies the renowned King Arthur, with Guinevere his second wife, in the island of Avalon'. Later, however, William Camden gave a reading which omits any reference to Guinevere; he includes a wood-cut of the cross in the sixth edition of his *Britannia* (1607), which he says was drawn from the 'first copy in the Abbey of Glastonbury', which might be thought to imply that it was not the original find of 1190. In fact the lettering depicted in Camden's engraving corresponds neither with forms of the fifth and sixth centuries, nor with those of the twelfth, but best compares with that on late Anglo-Saxon coinage. Possibly it should be ascribed to the period of Dunstan's refoundation of the monastery in the tenth century. Dunstan was responsible for extensive re-building at Glastonbury; his new cloister cut into the old monastic cemetery, which he levelled and re-walled. There is evidence that the early mausoleum was destroyed at this time, and perhaps a re-interment took place then. The apparent secrecy suggested by the fact that the name Arthur was never mentioned at this time, might be reflected in the cross having been found with its inscription hidden against the stone.

There is no reason to doubt the actual report of a twelfth-century exhumation. Excavation has shown that between the presumed site of the two standing stone crosses, a large irregular hole had been dug out and then shortly afterwards refilled in the 1180s or 90s. The evidence for this precise dating is found in the occurence in the hole of masons' chippings of Doulting stone, which was then first used at Glastonbury— in rebuilding the Lady Chapel in 1184-89. The bottom of the hole had disturbed two (or possibly three) of the slab-lined graves belonging to the earliest phase of the Celtic cemetery.

The remains found in 1190 were taken up and placed in the treasury of the abbey church. Later, at Easter in 1278 the remains were translated in the presence of Edward I and Queen Eleanor. The bones had

Figure 11   Camden's drawing of the Glastonbury lead cross, 1607.

been placed in two separate caskets, painted with the likenesses and the arms of Arthur and Guinevere. The marks of the fatal wound in Arthur's skull were pointed out; then the bones were wrapped in costly silks and moved for a second time to a new tomb before the high altar—although the skulls were retained on view outside the tomb for popular veneration. This new tomb survived into the sixteenth century when Leland saw it; but it was destroyed at the Reformation and the bones dispersed. The base of the cavity, lined with fine ashlar, was revealed by excavation in 1931.

44

By Leland's time the Arthurian locations were already firmly established in popular belief. He was shown, for instance, on the River Brue just a mile from the abbey 'a bridge of stone of a four arches communely caullid Pontperlus, wher men fable that Arture cast in his swerd'. This stone bridge replaced a wooden structure, the oak piles and paved approach of which were discovered in 1881.

The success of the Arthurian venture seems to have led to further demands of an archaeological nature. In the fourteenth century as one reflex of the growing interest in the Grail legends, the tradition that the Gospel had been brought to England by Joseph of Arimathea achieved great currency; and Edward III supported a divinely inspired search at Glastonbury for the original tomb of St Joseph. The remains were reported to have been discovered in 1367, and removed to a shrine in the Lady Chapel, so redoubling its prominence as a place of pilgrimage. The enrichment of the abbey continued throughout medieval times and at the Dissolution in 1539 it was still the wealthiest foundation in England, its immense church, now a mere ruin, finally attaining an overall length of some 550 feet. Its history ends with the execution of the obstinate Richard Whiting, sixty-first and last abbot of Glastonbury, high up on the Tor overlooking the abbey and the town. The site was extensively quarried for local building, and now very little remains of the once magnificent monastery.

*   *   *

Apart from the site of the abbey itself, two other Glastonbury locations have Arthurian associations: Glastonbury Tor, and Beckery, lying on a ridge of land extending from the remote westernmost edge of the island.

Both William of Malmesbury and John of Glastonbury describe traditions of Beckery going back to the fifth century. In particular they tell of a visit of the Irish saint Bridget to Glastonbury in 488, and how she spent some time at Beckery where there was an oratory dedicated to Mary Magdalene. There, after her return to Ireland in due course, she left certain personal relics, notably: a wallet, string of beads, hand-bell and some weaving tools; all of which were apparently still to be seen there as late as the fifteenth century.

John of Glastonbury records another story—a localised version of that which recurs in the romance *Perceval li Gallois*. King Arthur, resting at the nearby convent of Wearyall, is told in a dream by an angel to go to the hermitage of St Mary Magdalene at Beckery. There, *inter alia*, the king's attendant is slain in the act of stealing a gold candlestick. Nevertheless, a vision of the Virgin Mary with the infant Jesus appears to Arthur in the chapel at Beckery, and the king receives from the Virgin a crystal cross. It is in consequence of this that Arthur changes his armorial bearings to that of a silver cross on a green field with an image of the Virgin and Child in the right hand corner. The cross was said to be kept under guard in the abbey treasury in John's time; and he has heard that the gold candlestick stolen by Arthur's attendant was to be seen in the royal treasury at Westminster.

Whatever might lie behind either of these two stories, excavation has revealed a probably early origin for the religious foundation at Beckery. Around the foundations of the later medieval chapel were found traces of wattle-and-daub buildings which may have been similar to those belonging to the earliest phase of the Abbey site, although no coherent plan was recoverable. It is not impossible that at least some of these should have belonged to the post-Roman centuries, since they had been disturbed by grave-digging dating from mid-Saxon times. No datable material was found, although fragments of Mediterranean amphorae have been reported in association with a wattle-and-daub building just 60 yards away at The Mount. To the east of the chapel a ditch had been dug 3 feet deep and up to 4 feet across, apparently cutting the Beckery ridge off from the main island, and possibly representing a nominal *vallum monasterii*.

More explicit evidence for early post-Roman occupation comes from Glastonbury Tor—a dramatic hill rising to over 500 feet, composed of hard Jurassic limestone capped by a mass of sandstone. Relatively precipitous on three sides, to north, east and south, the summit is best approached by the less steep western slope, up from the direction of the Abbey. The summit itself is fairly flat—a roughly oval area about 100 by 50 feet. Its centre was apparently levelled for the later medieval church of St Michael, of which only the fifteenth-century tower now remains. The surface has been considerably disturbed, both by natural fissures and by human activity down to recent times (including the burial there of the eccentric John Rawls, *ob*. 1741). As a result, archaeological investigation and interpretation in the 60s was difficult. Traces of timber buildings were found on level platforms cut into the rock surface on the south and east sides of the summit, fairly sheltered from the prevailing south-westerlies. But insufficient remained to allow any kind of plan to be recovered. There were plentiful signs of fire, and an enormous quantity of animal bones—including joints of beef, mutton

46

and pork; while sherds of Mediterranean amphorae suggest that the occupants drank imported wine. Crucibles and hearths supplied evidence for metal-working on the summit; and it is not impossible that the most remarkable small find from the site—a bronze mount in the form of a helmeted head—should actually have been made on the Tor.

The essay *de Antiquitate Glastoniensis Ecclesiae*, wrongly attributed to William of Malmesbury, records a tradition that the Tor had been visited by St Patrick who, with one companion, spent three months

Figure 12   Bronze escutcheon from Glastonbury Tor (scale 1:1).

fasting in the ruin of an ancient chapel he found there. Upon being admonished in a vision to return to the Abbey, they decide that henceforth two members of the community should permanently reside on the Tor for the purpose of serving the chapel. But while the inaccessible, exposed character of the site might suggest its suitability for a hermitage, the total lack of water supply makes this less likely; while the evidence for abundant meat-eating scarcely fits with what we know of eremitical Celtic asceticism.

On the other hand, the Tor is naturally defensible and would be ideally suited as a small military outpost or signalling station. It is certainly possible that the Tor site should represent the stronghold of a petty local chieftain. If this interpretation is correct, then we might even guess at the name of the chieftain concerned. Arthur's connection with the Isle of Glastonbury is first recorded in the *Life of Gildas* written by Caradoc of Llancarfan about 1150. Caradoc tells the story of how Arthur's queen Guinevere had been abducted (*violatam et raptam*) by Melwas, king of Somerset (*Aestiva Regio*), and held captive at Glastonbury. After a long search Arthur gathers the forces of Devon and Cornwall, and comes to Glastonbury to do battle. Peace is brought about by the intervention of Gildas, together with the abbot and clergy of Glastonbury. Guinevere is restored; and both Arthur and Melwas come to worship in the Abbey church, and endow the foundation with estates. If the story told by Caradoc has any factual basis, then the Tor would form the only reasonable locale for the action, making perfect sense as the stronghold of Melwas where Guinevere was held and which was beseiged by Arthur.

V

CADBURY-CAMELOT

THE LARGE hillfort at South Cadbury in south Somerset occupies a steep-sided free-standing hill some 500 feet high, composed principally of the same Jurassic series which formed Glastonbury Tor eleven miles to the north-west: a hard limestone capped with hard yellow sandstone. To the west there are wide views across the low-lying Somerset Levels in the hinterland—the earlier flooding of which must have brought navigable waters relatively close to the hill. And away to the east a scarp marks the beginning of the chalk uplands of Wessex.

Human occupation of the hilltop seems to have started in Neolithic times. From the fifth century B.C. onwards it was fortified by stages until on the eve of the Roman invasion it formed a particularly impressive hillfort, its already steep sides defended by no less than four or five massive ramparts. And although now heavily wooded, the banks degraded and the ditches partially silted up, these defences are still formidable, with a slope of about 35 degrees. Camden spoke of it as 'a steepe hill, and hard to get up, (with) ditches so steepe that a man shall sooner slide downe, than goe down'. Despite its height, however, the profile of the hill is such that its summit is relatively windless. The inner rampart encloses an area of about 18 acres. There were two entrances: one on the north-east and one in the south-west. There is evidence that, as at Maiden Castle in Dorset, the Iron Age occupation came to an abrupt and violent end shortly after the date of the Roman invasion of 43 A.D. Presumably this was one of the native *oppida* stormed by Vespasian, future emperor, and then the general responsible for the subjugation of the south and west. The defences were partly dismantled, and thereafter the fort seems to have lain derelict for about two centuries. Then some time in the third or fourth century there is once more evidence of renewed human activity, apparently in the form of visits to a Romano-Celtic temple built there—possibly reviving an ancient pre-Roman cult. Traces of a timber shrine were found, together with several pits containing votive deposits. Subsequent to the collapse of Roman rule in the south-west, in the fifth and sixth centuries there is once again evidence for large-scale occupation of the hillfort marked by finds of imported Mediterranean pottery. The defences were repaired and major timber buildings constructed in the interior.

The association of South Cadbury hillfort with King Arthur is an ancient one. Already by the early sixteenth century it seems to have been believed locally that this was the hollow hill in which Arthur lay sleeping until the moment for his return. And probably already too, the site of Arthur's well was shown, and the lane where Arthur as leader of the wild hunt took his horse to drink. No doubt some degree

Figure 13 Sketches of Cadbury-Camelot from Musgrave's *Antiquitates Britanno–Belgicae*, 1719.

of self-generation is involved in this sort of folk-lore. But one element is significant. On a visit to Somerset in 1532, the King's Antiquary John Leland, remarks: 'at the very south ende of the chirche of South-Cadbyri standith Camallate, sumtyme a famose toun or castelle', adding 'The people can tell nothing ther but that they have hard say that Arture much resortid to Camalat'. Probably Leland knew the first printed edition of Ptolemy's *Cosmographia*, which shows a place called Camudulanum near here. Certainly, like Camden rather later, he was impressed by the fact that near the foot of the hill ran the river Cam or Camel, and that nearby lay the villages of Queen Camel and West Camel, which both call simply Camalet. Camden assures us that the local people referred to the hill as 'Arthur's Palace', although with no mention of the name Camalot itself. And it is curious that the eighteenth-century antiquary William Stukeley emphasised the fact that in his day the country people were ignorant of this particular name. While it is clear that the place-name Camel is of British origin, its exact etymology is uncertain. Perhaps it should be related to Welsh *cant*, 'enclosure' or 'host, party'; possibly it contains the name of Camulos, the Celtic god of war. As the name for King Arthur's court, Camalot first appears in Chretien's *Lancelot*, and may represent an Anglo-French invention. It is not impossible that the similarity between the two names should be mere coincidence. Nevertheless, in view of the now well-established local tradition, the title Cadbury-Camelot is a convenient coinage to distinguish this particular hillfort from several others of the same name in the West Country.

The recognition in the 1950s of fragments of imported Mediterranean pottery, collected from the surface of the interior of the hillfort after ploughing, led archaeologists once again to consider the Arthurian identification of the site with greater seriousness. These finds were in themselves remarkable in that this was at once the most easterly and furthest inland site to produce pottery of Tintagel type. From 1966-70 there took place a well-financed and superbly organised large-scale excavation of the site, using the most up-to-date methods of modern archaeology.

Important structural discoveries were made both in respect of the defences and the interior of the fort. The large area involved made the likelihood of discovering significant buildings on the eighteen-acre summit plateau seem remote. But extensive stripping led to the location of an important complex of buildings of different dates, and at least one sizeable timber structure. Occupying a central position in the in-

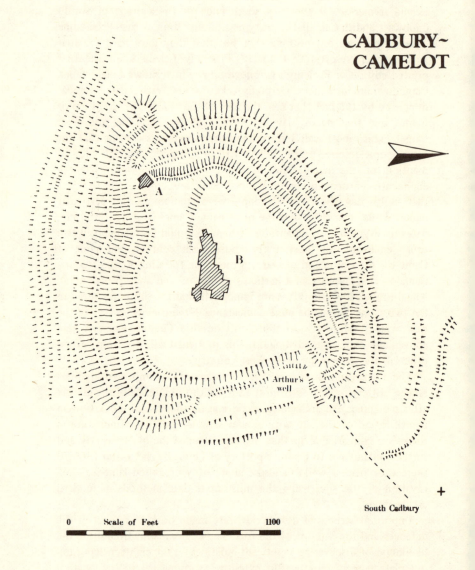

CADBURY~ CAMELOT

Arthur's well

South Cadbury

0   Scale of Feet   1100

Figure 14   Cadbury-Camelot: schematic plan of earthworks showing position of sites A and B.

terior were found the postholes of an aisled hall 63 x 34 feet, similar in size to the smaller of the two halls at Castle Dore. It was divided by an internal partition about one-third of the way from the east end. And probably the door lay adjacent to this screen, in the middle of one long side of the hall. Its more regular plan and shallower postholes suggest that this may have been more finely built than either of the halls at Castle Dore, relying more on skilful carpentry than earth-fast posts. As at Castle Dore, the floor levels, together with any hearth, had been obliterated by ploughing. But the building could be securely dated to the 'Arthurian' period on the evidence of pottery, both generally scattered and sealed in the structure: pieces of a freshly broken amphora had been tamped in round the foundation of the internal screen. Both its general character and its central position suggest that this hall will have been the principal building in the fort. And it must be assumed that various ancillary buildings were ranged round this. Although several rectangular six- and four-post buildings were located nearby, none can be assigned to the period of the hall with any confidence. But just four yards to the north of the hall lay the wall-trenches of a small rectangular building 13 x 6 feet, which a distinct concentration of imported pottery fragments suggests may represent the hall kitchen. In the event, only a small part of the interior was stripped and probably other buildings remain to be located elsewhere on the plateau.

While the main archaeological effort was concentrated on the interior, the south-western entrance of the fort was investigated, and traces were recovered from which it is possible to reconstruct its probable appearance in the 'Arthurian' period. Entrance through the perimeter defence seems to have been by way of a cobbled roadway, ten feet across, which passed through a timber-lined passage beneath a gate-tower raised on posts and tied in with the rampart and sentry walk-way either side. This passage was closed off at either end with fairly massive pairs of doors. The rampart itself took the form of a bank of rubble, which included large quantities of dressed masonry from derelict Roman buildings. Vertical gaps showed where stout wooden posts rose up the face to support some kind of breastwork on top of the bank, and there was presumably a timber-laced walkway or fighting platform behind. This style of building represents a reversion to a pre-Roman Celtic technique of fortification, similar to that found along the Rhenish *limes* at this date.

Although the outer lines of the defences were only examined in a single section, this evidence from the inner rampart alone seems to in-

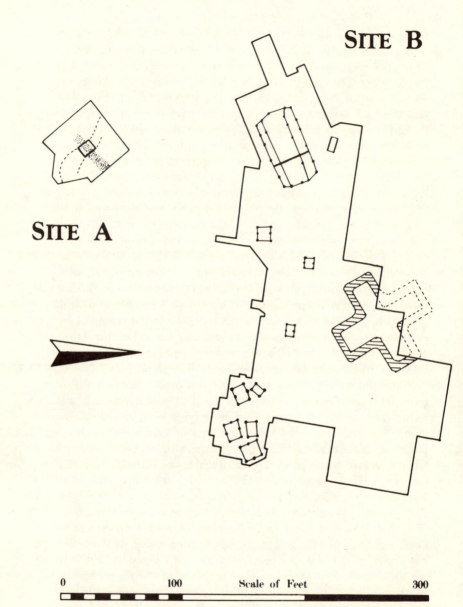

SITE B

SITE A

0   100   Scale of Feet   300

Figure 15   Cadbury-Camelot: schematic plan of site A, Arthurian-period gateway,
and site B, Arthurian-period hall with ancillary building, some possibly
associated four- and six-post structures, and foundation trench for cruciform ? church.

dicate nothing less than the construction of a new fortification. Certainly no other site of this period we know exhibits such a complete refurbishment of its main line of defence. But what sets Cadbury-Camelot apart from other Dark Age hillforts, whether re-occupied or newly built, is its sheer size. It would have been possible to fortify a much smaller area of the hilltop. At Garn Boduan (Caernarvonshire), for instance, the post-Roman defence of less than half an acre was constructed within a decayed Iron Age fort some 28 acres in extent. But at Cadbury it was decided to refortify the entire Iron Age perimeter of about twelve hundred yards. And the military and sociological implications of this decision are large. The comitatus of an individual prince, amounting to between, say, thirty and a hundred men, makes perfect sense in the context of a defended homestead like Castle Dore. But the ability both to construct and hold a fort of the magnitude of Cadbury-Camelot implies an altogether different scale. It demands an extensive organisation, and probably required the united resources of several British kingdoms at this date. Cadbury-Camelot must have been the base for an army that was large by the standards of the time, and the 'court' of a military leader of some status—a *dux bellorum*, and if not the historical Arthur, then an Arthur figure of some kind. It was admirably situated to form the base for campaigns against the West Saxon advance into the Upper Thames basin in the opening years of the sixth century. And whether or not a force from Cadbury-Camelot was involved in the victory at Mons Badonicus, it is clear that this fort must have played a strategic role in the Germano-Celtic confrontation in southern Britain in the late fifth to early sixth century.

The end of this post-Roman phase of occupation is shrouded in mystery. There is no evidence either for the fort's slow decline, or for its sudden and violent end. We know that the south-western entrance was being kept in repair as late as the second half of the sixth century, when a silver ring with Germanic animal ornament made some time about 550, and perhaps introduced into the fort either as loot or by a hostage, was lost beneath a second well-laid cobble resurfacing of the road through the south-western gateway. Possibly this refurbishment should be seen as a response to the renewed West Saxon expansion which led to the Battle of Deorham in 577, and marked the beginning of the end for the Celtic west.

Once again the hilltop was abandoned, this time for some four centuries, until at the beginning of the eleventh century in the reign of Aethelred, the fort enjoyed a brief reflorescence as the site of a late

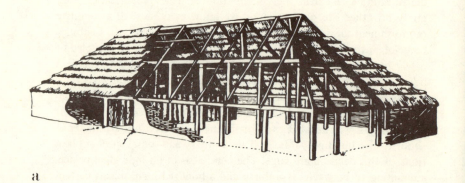

a

b

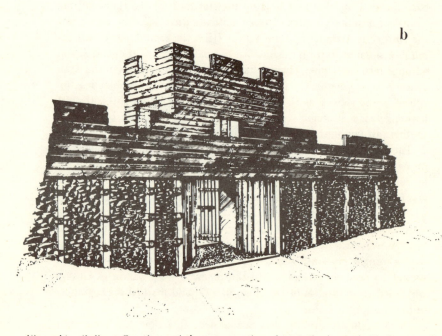

Figure 16   Cadbury-Camelot: artist's reconstruction of (a) Arthurian-period hall
and (b) gate-tower.

Saxon *burh*, and the location of a royal mint. The gateways were finely rebuilt in stone; and at the same time probably, on top of the summit the plan seems to have been laid out for what should probably be interpreted as a fine cruciform church. But neither this nor any other building seems actually to have been constructed. For shortly after the viking Cnut's accession in 1017, the *burh* was abandoned and the hilltop once more given up to cultivation and the plough.

VI

SELECT BIBLIOGRAPHY

1 THE 'ARTHURIAN' WEST

ANON	*La Vie de Saint Samson*, ed. R. Fawtier, Paris 1912. Transl. by T. Taylor, *The Life of St Sampson of Dol*, London, 1925.
ASHE, G.	(Ed.) *The Quest for Arthur's Britain*, London, 1968.
BOWEN, E. G.	*Saints, Seaways and Settlements in the Celtic Lands*, Cardiff, 1969.
BRANIGAN, K.	'The End of Roman West', *Trans. Bristol and Glos. Antiqu. Soc.*, XCI (1972), 117-28.
CHADWICK, N.	'The Colonization of Brittany from Celtic Britain', *Proc. British Academy*, LI (1965), 235-99.
FOWLER, P. J.	'Hillforts, A.D. 400-700', *The Iron Age and its Hillforts*, ed. D. Hill and M. Jesson, Southampton, 1971, pp. 203-13.
FOX, A. and C.	'Wansdyke Reconsidered', *Archaeological Journal*, CXV (1958), 1-48.
FOX, C.	*The Personality of Britain*, 4th ed. Cardiff, 1952.
HAYES, J. W.	*Late Roman Pottery*, London, 1972.
JENNER, H.	'The Irish Immigrations into Cornwall in the late Fifth and early Sixth Centuries', *Royal Cornwall Polytechnic Soc., 84th Annual Report* (1917), 38-85.
MOORE, D.	(Ed.) *The Irish Sea Province in Archaeology and History*, Cardiff, 1970, espec. pp. 55-65.
PEARCE, S. M.	'The dating of some Celtic dedications and hagiographical traditions in South Western Britain', *Trans. Devonshire Assoc.*, CV (1973), 95-120.
	'The Cornish Elements in the Arthurian Tradition', *Folklore*, LXXXV (1974), 145-63.
PORTER, H. M.	*The Celtic Church in Somerset*, Bath, 1971.
RAHTZ, P. A. and FOWLER, P.	'Somerset A.D. 400-700', *Archaeology and the Landscape*, ed. P. Fowler, London, 1972, pp. 187-217.

RAVENHILL, W. L. D.	'The Settlement of Devon in the Dark Ages', *Trans. Devonshire Assoc.*, LXXXVI (1954), 63-74.
	'The Settlement of Cornwall during the Celtic Period', *Geography*, XL (1955), 237-48.
SNELL, F. J.	*King Arthur's Country*, London, 1926.
STEVENS, C. E.	'A Lady of Quality from Roman Devonshire', *Trans. Devonshire Assoc.*, LXXXIV (1952), 172-77.
THOMAS, A. C.	'Cornwall in the Dark Ages', *Proc. West Cornwall Field Club*, II (1957-58), 59-72.
	'Imported Pottery in Dark Age Western Britain', *Medieval Archaeology*, III (1959), 89-111.
	'The Irish Settlements in Post-Roman Western Britain: a Survey of the Evidence', *Journal of the Royal Inst. of Cornwall*, NS. VI (1972), 251-74.
	'Irish Colonists in south-west Britain', *World Archaeology*, V (1973), 5-13.
TURNER, A. G. C.	'Some Aspects of Celtic Survival in Somerset', *Proc. Somerset Arch. and Nat. Hist. Soc.*, XCVII (1952), 148-51.

2   TINTAGEL

ANON	*Le haut livre du Graal, Perlesvaus*, ed. W. A. Nitze et al, Chicago, 1932. Transl. by S. Evans, *The High History of the Holy Graal*, London, 1898.
BURROW, I. C. G.	'Tintagel—some problems', *Scottish Archaeological Forum*, V (1973), 99-103.
CRAIK, H.	'In King Arthur's Land', *Good Words,* Jan. 1, 1867, 61-71.
GEOFFREY OF MONMOUTH	*Historia Regum Britanniae*, ed. A. Schulz, Halle, 1854. Transl. by L. Thorpe, *History of the Kings of Britain*, Harmondsworth, 1966.
JENNER, H.	'Tintagel Castle in History and Romance', *Journal of the Royal Inst. of Cornwall*, XXII (1927), 190-200.
RADFORD, C. A. R.	'Tintagel: the Castle and Celtic Monastery; Interim Report', *Antiquaries Journal*, XV (1935), 401-19.
	Tintagel Castle, 2nd ed. London, 1939.
	'Tintagel in History and Legend', *Journal of the Royal Inst. of Cornwall*, LXXXVI (1942), Appendix 25-41.

'Imported Pottery found at Tintagel, Cornwall', *Dark Age Britain*, ed. D. B. Harden, London, 1956, pp. 59-70.

'The Celtic Monastery in Britain', *Archaeologia Cambrensis*, CXI (1962), 1-24.

THOMAS, A. C.   'Rostat, Rosnat*, and the early Irish Church', *Eriu*, XXII (1971), 100-6.

3   CASTLE DORE AND THE TRISTAN STONE

BEROUL   *The Romance of Tristran*, ed. A. Ewart, Oxford, 1939-70. Transl. by A. S. Fedrick, Harmondsworth, 1970.

BROMWICH, R.   'Some remarks on the Celtic sources of "Tristan"', *Y Cymmrodor*, 1953, 32-60.

JENNER, H.   'The Tristan Romance and its Cornish Provenance', *Journal of the Royal Inst. of Cornwall*, XIX (1912-14), 464-88.

LOTH, J.   *Contributions a l'étude des Romans de la Table Ronde*, Paris, 1912.

MACALISTER, R. A. S.   *Corpus Inscriptionum Insularum Celticarum*, Dublin, 1945-49.

RADFORD, C. A. R.   'Report on the Excavations at Castle Dore', *Journal of the Royal Inst. of Cornwall*, NS. I, (1951), Appendix, 1-119.

RAHTZ, P. A.   'Castle Dore—a reappraisal of the post-Roman structures', *Cornish Archaeology*, X (1971), 49-54.

ROWE, H.   'Tristram, King Rivalen and King Mark', *Journal of the Royal Inst. of Cornwall*, XXII (1928), 445-64.

WHITE, J. M.   'Tristan and Isolt', *History Today*, III (1953), 233-39.

WRMONOC   'Vie de Saint Paul de Leon en Bretagne', ed. C. Cuissard, *Revue Celtique*, V (1881-83), 413-60.

4   GLASTONBURY

ADAM OF DOMERHAM   *Historia de Rebus Gestis Glastoniensibus*, ed. T. Hearne, Oxford, 1727.

CARADOC OF LLANCARFAN   *Vita Gildae*, ed. T. Mommsen, M. G. H. Auct. Antiqu., III (1898), 107-10. Ed. and transl. by H. Williams, *Gildas*, London, 1899-1901, pp. 390-413.

DITMAS, E. M. R.	'The cult of Arthurian relics', *Folklore*, LXXV (1964), 19-33.
FINBERG, H. P. R.	'Ynyswitrin', in *Lucerna*, London, 1964, pp. 83-94.
GIRALDUS CAMBRENSIS	*Speculum Ecclesiae*, ed. J. S. Brewer, Rolls Series, London, 1873.
	De Principis Instructione, ed. G. F. Warner, Rolls Series, London, 1891.
JOHN OF GLASTONBURY	*Historia de Rebus Glastoniensibus*, ed. T. Hearne, Oxford, 1726.
JONES, W. A.	'On the reputed discovery of King Arthur's remains at Glastonbury', *Proc. Somerset Arch. and Nat. Hist. Soc.*, IX (1859), 128-41.
LELAND, J.	*Assertio Inclytissimi Arturii*, London, 1544. Transl. by R. Robinson, *The Assertion of King Arthur*, London, 1582.
LOT, F.	'Glastonbury et Avalon', *Romania*, XXVII (1898), 529-73.
NITZE, W. A.	'The exhumation of King Arthur at Glastonbury', *Speculum*, IX (1934), 355-61.
PEERS, C. R., CLAPHAM, A. W. and HORNE, E.	'Interim Report on the excavations at Glastonbury Abbey', *Antiquaries Journal*, X (1930), 24-29.
	'Glastonbury Abbey excavations, 1930-31', *Proc. Somerset Arch. and Nat. Hist. Soc.*, LXXVII (1931), 83-6.
RADFORD, C. A. R.	'Excavations at Glastonbury Abbey, 1951', *Antiquity*, XXV (1951), 213; and subsequent interim reports: *ibid.*, XXVII (1953), 41; XXIX (1955), 33-4; XXXI (1957), 171; *Notes and Queries for Somerset and Dorset*, XXVII (1955), 21-5; (1957), 68-73, 165-69; (1960), 251-55; (1961), 123, XXVIII (1963), 114-17; (1965), 211-13, 235-36.
	'The Church in Somerset down to 1100', *Proc. Somerset Arch. and Nat. Hist. Soc.*, CVI (1962), 28-45.
RAHTZ, P. A.	'Excavations on Glastonbury Tor, Somerset, 1964-66', *Archaeological Journal*, CXXVII (1970), 1-81.
RAHTZ, P. A. and HIRST, S.	*Beckery Chapel, Glastonbury, 1967-68*, Glastonbury, 1974.
ROBINSON, J. A.	*Somerset Historical Essays*, London, 1921.
	Two Glastonbury Legends, Cambridge, 1926.
ROBINSON, J. L.	'St Brigid and Glastonbury', *Journal of the Royal Society of Antiquaries of Ireland*, LXXXIII (1953), 97-9.

SCHOFIELD, A. N. E. D.   'St Patrick at Glastonbury', *Irish Ecclesiastical Record,*
                          5thS. CVII (1967), 345-61.

SLOVER, C. H.   'William of Malmesbury and the Irish', *Speculum,* II
                          (1927), 268-83.

WILLIAM OF   *De Rebus Gestis Regum Anglorum,* ed. W. Stubbs,
MALMESBURY   Rolls Series XC, London, 1887. Transl. by J. Steven-
                          son, *Church Historians of England,* III, London, 1854.

PSEUDO WILLIAM   *De Antiquitate Glastoniensis Ecclesiae,* ed. J-P. Migne,
OF MALMESBURY   *Patrologia Latina,* CLXXIX, 1681-1734. Transl. by F.
                          Lomax, *The Antiquities of Glastonbury,* London,
                          1908.

5   CADBURY-CAMELOT

ALCOCK, L.   'A reconnaissance excavation at South Cadbury Castle,
                          Somerset, 1966', *Antiquaries Journal,* XLVII (1967),
                          70-6; and subsequent interim reports: *ibid.,* XLVIII
                          (1968), 6-17; XLIX (1969), 30-40; L (1970), 14-25;
                          LI (1971), 1-7; and in a rather more popular form:
                          Antiquity XLI (1967), 50-3; XLII (1968), 47-51; XLIII
                          (1969), 52-6; XLIV (1970), 46-9; XLVI (1972), 29-38.

                          'By South Cadbury is that Camelot . . .', London,
                          1972.

BENNETT, J. A.   'Camelot', *Proc. Somerset Arch. and Nat. Hist. Soc.,*
                          XXVI (1890), 1-19.

GRAY, H. S-G.   'Trial excavations at Cadbury Castle, S. Somerset,
                          1913', *ibid.,* LIX (2) (1913), 1-24.

HARFIELD, M.   'Cadbury Castle', *ibid.,* CVI (1962), 62-5.

JONES, T.   'A sixteenth century version of the Arthurian Cave
                          legend', *Studies in Language and Literature in Honour
                          of Margaret Schlauch,* ed. M. Brahmer, et al., Warsaw,
                          1966, pp. 175-85.

RADFORD, C. A. R. and   'Cadbury Castle, South Cadbury', *Proc. Somerset
COX, J. A.   Arch. and Nat. Hist. Soc.,* XCIX-C (1954-55), 106-13.

THOMAS, C.   'Are these the walls of Camelot?', *Antiquity,* XLIII
                          (1969), 27-30.

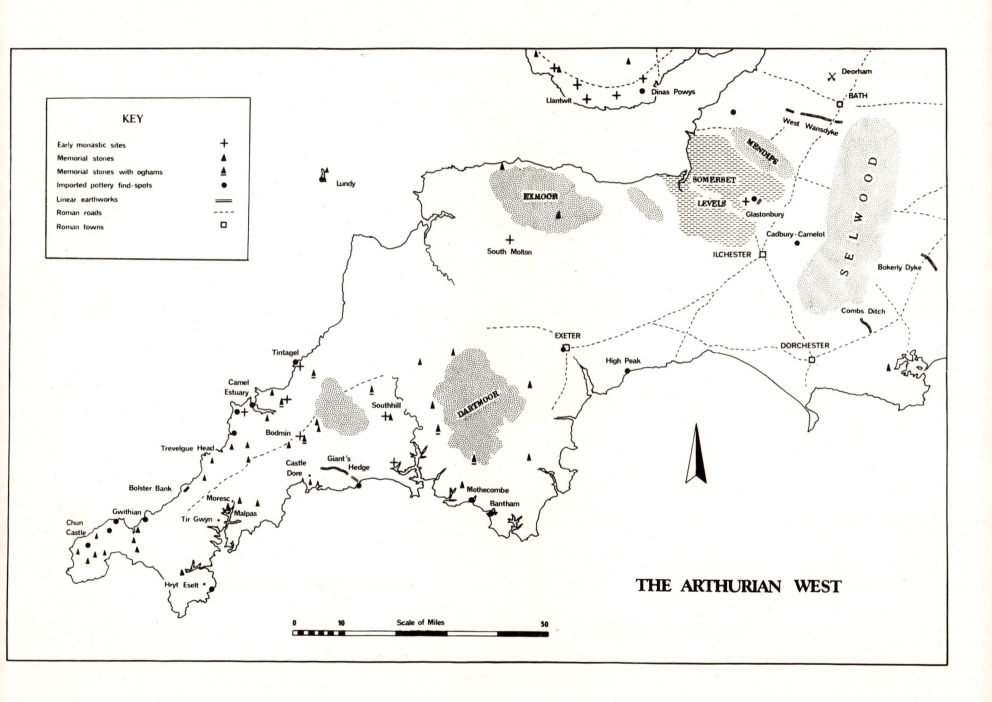

KEY

Early monastic sites   +
Memorial stones   ▲
Memorial stones with oghams   ▲
Imported pottery find-spots   ●
Linear earthworks   ═══
Roman roads   ‒ ‒ ‒
Roman towns   ▫

Deorham

Llantwit   Dinas Powys

BATH

West Wansdyke

MENDIPS

SOMERSET

LEVELS

Glastonbury

Cadbury - Camelot

SELWOOD

ILCHESTER

Bokerly Dyke

Lundy

EXMOOR

South Molton

Combs Ditch

EXETER

DORCHESTER

High Peak

Tintagel

Camel
Estuary

Southhill

DARTMOOR

Bodmin

Trevelgue Head

Castle
Dore

Giant's
Hedge

Mothecombe

Bolster Bank

Bantham

Chun
Castle

Moresc

Gwithian

Malpas

Tir Gwyn

Hryt Eselt

THE ARTHURIAN WEST

0   10   Scale of Miles   50